Wild Animals

POLAR BEAR

Lionel Bender

Chrysalis Children's Books

First published in the UK in 2004 by
Chrysalis Children's Books
An imprint of Chrysalis Books Group Plc,
The Chrysalis Building, Bramley Road,
London W10 6SP

ISBN 1 84458 171 3

British Library Cataloguing in Publication Data
for this book is available from the British Library.

Editorial Manager *Joyce Bentley*
Senior Editor *Rasha Elsaeed*
Editorial Assistant *Camilla Lloyd*

Produced by Bender Richardson White
Project Editor *Lionel Bender*
Designer *Ben White*
Production *Kim Richardson*
Picture Researcher *Cathy Stastny*
Cover Make-up *Mike Pilley, Radius*

Printed in China

10 9 8 7 6 5 4 3 2

Words in **Bold** can be found in New words on page 31.

Typography *Natascha Frensch*
Read Regular, READ SMALLCAPS and Read Space; European Community Design Registration 2003
and Copyright © Natascha Frensch 2001-2004 **Read Medium**, **Read Black** and *Read Slanted*
Copyright © Natascha Frensch 2003-2004

Picture credits
Cover © Digital Vision.
© Digital Vision pages 1, 2, 4, 7, 8, 14, 16, 19, 22, 23, 24, 25. © Corbis Images Inc.: pages 5 (Dan Guravich),
17 (W. Perry Conway), 28 (Jeff Vanuga), 29 (Jeff Vanuga). © Frank Lane Picture Agency Limited: pages 6
(David Hosking), 11 (Michael Gore), 12 (Fritz Polking), 15 (F. Lanting/Minden Pictures), 18 (Terry Andrewartha),
20 (Terry Andrewartha), 26 (E. & D. Hosking), 27 (C. Carvalho).

Contents

Polar bears

Polar bears are the largest land animals that hunt for their food.

Male polar bears are bigger and stronger than the females.

Home

The polar bear lives on the land and frozen seas around the **North Pole**.

This part of the world is called
the Arctic. It is cold there all
year round.

Food

The polar bear's main food is seals. It hunts for them on the ice and in the sea.

A polar bear will also eat walrus, reindeer and berries.

Hunting

A hungry polar bear creeps up on its **prey**. Then it chases and grabs the animal.

Seabirds try to steal some of the polar bear's catch.

Daily life

This polar bear is sleeping. It spends most of the day resting.

Polar bears can travel long distances each day to find food.

Senses

Polar bears' most important **sense** is smell. They sniff the air for the **scent** of prey.

A polar bear has good hearing
and eyesight.

Weapons

A polar bear has long **claws**.
It uses them in fights over food
or in battles for a **mate**.

Its teeth are mostly used for crushing the bones of its prey.

Skin and fur

A polar bear is covered with woolly fur and hair. This keeps the bear warm in the snow.

Thick fat under the skin keeps the polar bear warm in water.

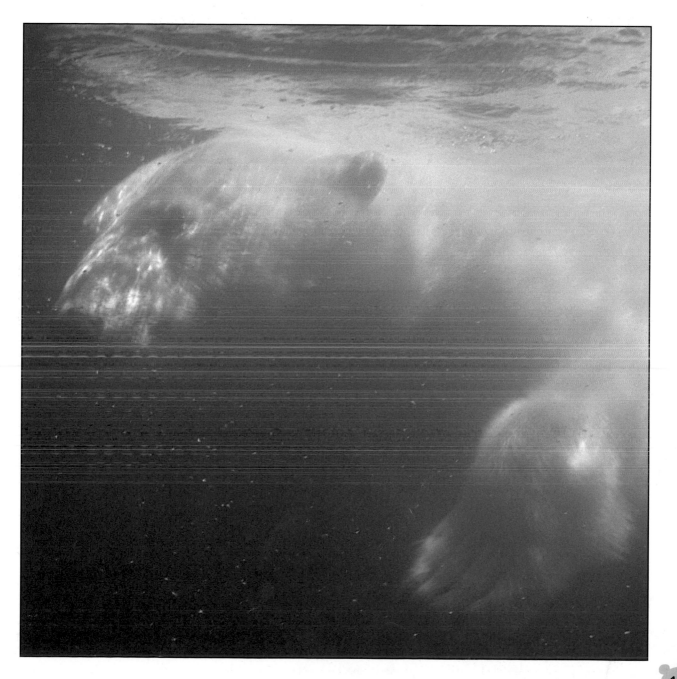

Family life

A mother polar bear digs a **den** under the snow. The babies come out of the den in spring.

Baby polar bears are called cubs.
They feed on their mother's milk.

Growing up

Young polar bears grow quickly. Their mother looks after them and teaches them how to hunt.

They stay with their mother until they are two years old.

Becoming an adult

Polar bears reach their full size when they are four or five years old.

Adult polar bears live on their own. They meet only to **breed**.

In danger

The Arctic ice is slowly melting.
There is less ice for polar bears
to hunt and to breed on.

Some people kill polar bears for their skins. They use them to make coats and rugs.

Polar bear care

Sometimes polar bears enter villages. Wildlife carers catch the bears to help them survive.

The bears are lifted by helicopter and taken back to their home, safe in the wild.

Quiz

1 Where do polar bears live?

2 What is the weather like in a polar bear's home?

3 Why do polar bears travel long distances each day?

4 What keeps a polar bear warm?

5 What are baby polar bears called?

6 At what age do young polar bears leave their mothers?

7 At what age do polar bears reach full size?

8 Why are polar bears in danger?

The answers are all in this book!

New words

breed a male and female animal getting together
to make babies.

claws long, curved fingernails and toenails.

den shelter where mother gives birth to babies
and looks after them. Polar bears make their dens
deep in snow.

mate a male or female animal with which to breed.

North Pole an area of snow and ice on the Earth
to which the North end of a compass needle points.

prey an animal that is hunted and killed for food.

scent smell.

sense the way animals find out about their
surroundings Animals have five senses – sight,
hearing, smell, taste and touch. The body senses
something when it notices it is there.

Index